The Still Waters of Beauty

# The Still Waters
# of Beauty

*Augustine of Hippo*

*Edited by*

*Oliver Davies*

*Translations by*

*Adrian Roberts and Oliver Davies*

*with an introduction by*

## Angela Ashwin

New City
London   Dublin   Edinburgh

First published in Great Britain 1993
by
New City
57 Twyford Avenue, London W3 9PZ

© 1993 New City

*Translations by*
*Adrian Roberts and Oliver Davies*

*Cover design by Duncan Harper*

British Cataloguing in Publication Data
A catalogue record for this book is
available from the British Library

ISBN 0 904287 47 5

Typeset in Great Britain
by
Phoenix Typesetting,
Ilkley, West Yorkshire

Printed and bound in Great Britain
by
The Cromwell Press, Broughton Gifford, Wiltshire

# Series Preface

*We have been long familiar with the achievement of the Fathers of the Church in terms of Christian theology and doctrine, and no one can make a serious study of the Christian faith without reading the great texts of the patristic age and following their far-reaching debates. But it is not this aspect of the Fathers' achievement which this series aims to explore. Rather, our wish is to rediscover something of the personal conviction and the deep spiritual vision which is luminously present in a considerable number of patristic works, which have for too long been neglected in favour of other writings which are of historical and theological importance. But, according to the good patristic maxim, the best theology is written by those who most deeply conform their lives to God.*

*Any of the Church Fathers would be baffled by the explosion of spiritual writing that we find in the modern age; the term 'spirituality' itself is a relatively recent invention. Their world was one in which theology, the faith as expressed in the creeds and spiritual experience formed a single unity in which each element was dependent on the others. The same, alas, cannot be said of us, and the surge of interest in spirituality must be seen as being, in part, an attempt to reclaim this original unity for ourselves.*

*There is much in the spiritual writings of the Fathers which is timeless. Indeed, it is astonishing how fresh and topical much of what they wrote can seem today, despite the gulf that exists between their world of late antiquity and our own world of advancing technology and mass communication. Perhaps it is human nature itself which is timeless, though there are in addition subtle points of contact between the emergent Christianity of the ancient world and our own age in which the Churches must discover their own roots in order to weather the onslaughts of secularism.*

The Spirituality of the Fathers *contains carefully chosen selections from the often lesser known spiritual writings of the Fathers, newly rendered into a modern idiom, in order to set before the public the great spiritual treasures of patristic literature. It is our hope that this will strengthen the Christian life of the Spirit in our own times, and that we may come to share in that living faith more fully, which the Fathers, in their own age, always defended and fostered, by their work and their prayer.*

# *Contents*

| | |
|---|---|
| Series Preface | 5 |
| Introduction by Angela Ashwin | 9 |
| Augustine of Hippo: His Life and Works | 29 |
| Short Bibliography | 33 |
| Selections from *Exposition of the Psalms* | 35 |

# Introduction

Ask a random group of Christians what they think about St Augustine of Hippo, and the responses you get may be anything from, 'He told his story in some frank *Confessions*,' to 'He had a mother who was really persistent! She never gave up following him around and praying for his conversion!' or even 'Isn't he the one who taught that the material world is evil?'

Augustine has received rather a bad press lately, especially among those rightly affirming the essential goodness of God's creation. It is true that Augustine's doctrine of a fallen humanity hardened in his later life, during the turbulent days after the collapse of the Roman Empire. But he did have a strong sense of the beauty and wonder of creation, and believed that it was good for biblical scholars to study some geography and natural science[1]. It would be a pity if our hesitations about Augustine were to blind us to the many good things in his writings.

Most of us are already indebted to Augustine in those sayings of his which have become well-known prayers,

[1] In his work *On Christian Culture*.

such as, 'You have made us for yourself, O Lord, and our hearts are restless until they rest in you.' It may seem surprising that ordinary mortals like us can relate to this saint, considering that he was an intellectual genius and outstanding champion of the faith, living in a very different culture from our own. But his message about our human frailty and our need of God speaks to us now just as it will have spoken to Christians in the fourth and fifth centuries.

Indeed, I was delighted to find many homely and down to earth illustrations in this selection. Here is this theological giant likening God to a mother who briskly rubs clean her squawking infant in the bath tub (*Purification through suffering,* page 39). Augustine had had a child by his former mistress, and must have often watched this noisy domestic scene. In this passage he is at pains to point out that such mothers are 'full of affection' even when their children are still bawling, and he concludes that 'our God too is full of love,' even when we don't like the process of being purified by him. This is great stuff, and describes exactly how I have sometimes felt in the hands of God after I've made a mess of things and had to face up to my stupidity and be cleansed and forgiven.

When I began to read these commentaries, I wondered how to go about it. Should I start by looking at the psalm on which Augustine is reflecting, and then see what he has to say in the commentary? I tried this at first, but in the end I found it more helpful to work the other way round. So I would suggest to the reader that one possible way of using this book is to read through Augustine's text first, slowly and thoughtfully. If an idea or image strikes you, stay with it, and don't try to finish the section just for the sake of it. (God often seems to touch us through a thought in a piece of writing, so that we are helped to remain still with him for a while.) A passage may thus last you anything from five minutes to a few days. After reading Augustine's commentaries in this way, I found that the psalm itself often took on a new depth and richness. This approach to the book is just a suggestion; everyone will find his or her own way.

In a few cases you will see a variation between Augustine's version of a psalm and most of our modern prayer books and Bibles. This is because he was using a Latin version of the Greek Old Testament (the Septuagint), in which certain translations of the original Hebrew are different. I was amused by the way Augustine sometimes takes a word or phrase from a psalm and launches into something quite unconnected, such as a Gospel story or a teaching of St Paul. He does this because he regards the Old Testament as being full of hidden meaning pointing to Christ. Through all these writings, he shows us how his own life and prayer have been enriched from using and meditating on the psalms himself.

Augustine's images often seem to leap out of a piece of theological reflection, so that the page comes alive. For example, in *Poverty of spirit* (page 110), he wants to convey how feeble our own efforts at good behaviour are compared with God's infinite goodness. So he describes our virtues as

11

'merely spray' compared to 'that fountain of righteousness which softens our lives and melts the hardness of our wickedness'. I love the poetry in that sentence, which reminds me of the spasmodic squirtings of a garden insect spray compared with a magnificent and never-ending fountain. Augustine often uses images such as this to emphasize our human weakness, not because he wants to cast us into hopeless guilt and despair, but in order to encourage us to depend on God rather than on ourselves.

He knows from his own turbulent youth that we cannot overcome our selfish impulses by relying on our own resolutions and willpower. He is adamant that all the goodness in us is there by the gift and grace of God. Augustine spent much time and energy battling against people who seemed to think that we can achieve holiness and salvation by our own merit and effort. Not so, says Augustine. In a beautiful prayer arising from his thoughts on Psalm 71 he says, 'From my youth I have turned to you, God, and have been renewed by you. I was made by you, and then made a new creation. I was shaped by you, and then reformed. I learned that my merits counted for nothing, but that your grace came to me freely' (*New creation in God,* pp. 80–1). We could all benefit from praying those words.

Augustine's belief that we cannot deal with our sinfulness on our own permeates his writings, and is behind his description of the crowds eagerly flocking to the bloodthirsty sports at the amphitheatre (*God is more beautiful,* p. 58). This could be said to have a modern parallel in the lust for malicious gossip about public figures that is stirred up by some of our newspapers. We all share the responsibility, for we are all fascinated by what is crude and cruel, and allow ourselves to enjoy jokes or gossip at other people's expense. But Augustine is a good teacher. He doesn't just point out the problem. He also shows us what to do about it, encouraging us to turn to God and put all our hope in him. It is Jesus who makes this possible: 'Do not turn away from the cross of Christ. You shall not sink: hold fast to Christ!' (*Unite yourself to the eternity of God,* p. 98).

Augustine's reference to the amphitheatre reminds me of a story that he tells in his *Confessions.* When he was a young man, he had a friend called Alipius, who enjoyed going to watch gladiators fighting to the death at the arena. One day Augustine told his friend that he considered it to be thoroughly degrading to go to such brutal events. At this Alipius began to feel ashamed of his obsession with the sport, and resolved immediately to stop going.

Unfortunately Alipius had some wild friends, who, one night, dragged him unwillingly to the arena. But Alipius sat with his eyes tightly shut and steadfastly refused to be drawn into the excitement. His determination held out for a while. But at the end of a particularly savage contest, the crowd suddenly leapt to its feet in a wave of approval as one fighter was being hacked to bits. Alipius couldn't resist opening his eyes, even though he still intended to have nothing to do with it. But when he saw the gruesome spectacle below him, he was swept up into the general hysteria and started shouting for blood like everyone else. His shame afterwards was considerable!

At the end of this story, Augustine predictably comments that Alipius's mistake was to trust in his own strength to resist temptation.

I enjoyed Augustine's ingenious use of 'the moon' as a symbol of the Church in *An image of the Church* (page 37). The moon, he says, is like the Church because it sometimes appears to be mostly plunged into darkness. I'm sure many people would agree with that today! But there is hope, because the full moon always comes back, reflecting once more the light that has never stopped streaming in its direction. This analogy can also speak on a personal level to many of us whose spiritual life is for ever waxing and waning. We probably know times when we are somehow able to receive and reflect a bit of God's glory; but at other times, our pride and selfish preoccupations get in the way and darken the scene once more. Each of us is a microcosm of the whole Church, and there is hope for us as individuals, as well as for the whole body. Augustine's thoughts encourage and reassure me that we are not irrevocably stuck in the darkness when we go wrong, but that God is constantly turning us back to his light. 'The moon wanes in order to be renewed,' he says. Thank goodness for that.

I feel that a note of caution is needed over a few passages in this book, because Augustine uses some illustrations which are fine in certain circumstances, but which could be quite harmful in others. Take, for example, his thoughts about suffering on page 39. Alongside the gentler image of the baby in the bath tub there is a much harder one, of God as a surgeon. Augustine is assuming here that the pain which people are enduring is the result of their own folly. It often is, of course. Gossips become unpopular, gluttons become sick, and we all pay the price for polluting and ravaging our planet's resources. But I could not put this passage into the hands of a friend whose child had just died, and tell her, 'God is a surgeon, and there was something rotten in you which needed to be cut out.' I'm sure Augustine wouldn't have said this to such a person either. This shows how important it is not to pick out a snippet of teaching and try to apply it to every situation. We need to put this remark about human pain in the context of all his teachings.

Augustine does frequently affirm that innocent people suffer. And he does say that the unjust distribution of misery in the world is beyond our comprehension: 'Do not be disturbed by those who do evil and flourish in this world. "The thoughts of God are too deep for me to understand,"' (*Unite yourself to the eternity of God*, pp. 98-9). But further on in that passage I am again disturbed, because Augustine makes it sound so easy to endure suffering with patience. If you are worn out by a long illness or a difficulty that stretches out into the indefinite future, I don't imagine that you will be very impressed with the following words: 'You are thinking of your own short life. You want everything to be fulfilled during your few days upon earth. But . . . God will accomplish it in his own time. Why be weary and impatient? God is eternal.'

Hmm! If I am facing an acutely painful situation, I need to be able to explode to God first, before I can begin to express my faith that everything is ultimately in his hands. I need to shout out my 'No,' as Jesus did in Gethsemane, before I can step into the darkness with God and cling to a trust in the victory of love over evil and suffering.

Ultimately, we do need to face the truth of our situation, and surrender ourselves into God's hands. That is the truth Augustine is trying to teach us. But I think that the mysterious process of protesting *and* accepting, as we work through our pain, is more complicated than he seems to be suggesting here.

I can forgive Augustine for that particular passage, however, when I read his superb meditation on the verse from Psalm 91: 'He will cover you between his shoulders, and under his wings you will find hope,' (*God protects us,* pp. 95–6). Reflecting upon the tenderness of a mother hen with her chicks, Augustine says: 'The protection of God's extended wings keeps you between his shoulders, so that, enclosing you on both sides, they hold you between them . . . If a hen keeps her young safe under her wings, how much safer you will be under the wings of God.'

He then makes a link with Jesus's own words over Jerusalem, 'How often have I wanted to gather your children as a hen gathers her young,' and boldly observes that the hen is a comparatively weak and vulnerable bird, unable to fly away from the nest: 'We recognize the hen by the feebleness of her cry and the loosening of her feathers.' Augustine seems to realize that this is rather a shocking thing to say about God, and comments, almost with embarrassment: 'There is nothing dishonourable in the name of a hen!' He then skilfully applies all this to the incarnation: 'She [the hen] is completely changed by her love for her young. Because they are weak, she shares their weakness. And because we were feeble creatures, God's Wisdom made himself weak for our sakes.' This is a moving and inspiring passage, inviting us to surrender ourselves into the care of our vulnerable yet all protecting 'mother-hen' God.

For those of us who struggle to pray in the middle of a busy existence, Augustine has many good things to say. He assures us that all of life can become an act of praise, and that it is our *desire* for God that counts most. He questions whether it is possible to praise God all day long, and concedes that St Paul's injunction to 'pray without ceasing' is decidedly difficult. 'Are we to kneel, to bow low and to lift our hands continuously?' he asks *(Unceasing prayer,* p. 54). I certainly can't see myself falling to my knees in the supermarket or on a railway platform, but I do often want to pray more, and to be closer to God through the course of each day. Augustine's next remark is reassuring: 'The continuation of your longing is the continuation of your prayer.' That is to say, if we want to pray, we are already praying.

Augustine offers more advice on this theme. 'Whatever it is that you do, do it well, and you will have praised God,' *(All life is worship,* p. 43). These words would be most encouraging to busy people like an acquaintance of mine, a tired and overworked barrister, who wishes that he could be more consciously aware of God's presence during a day's work. He once told me, 'I can pray while gardening or washing the car – if I remember. But when I'm with a client or in court it's impossible, because I have to give all my attention to the task in hand.' But Augustine's belief that to do a job well is to praise God anyway, could set my friend free from much guilt and anxiety. As Augustine says, our intention and motive are what matters.

I like the image which he uses in the section *Praising God with the whole of your life* (page 123). He compares the intentions of our heart to a Roman Emperor on his throne, whose single edict can have vast consequences for a whole province. I find this a challenging reminder that each of my actions, however small, can have a profound effect on other people's lives. If we are going to have any hope of living in the way God wants, or of praising him with the whole of ourselves, Augustine insists that the 'emperor' on the throne of our hearts must be Christ himself. We owe a lot to Augustine for seeing that the 'heart' (where our deepest desires lie) is essential to any true knowledge of God. Intellect alone is not enough.

Augustine looks at many aspects of prayer in these commentaries. In *Calling upon God* (page 86) he tackles the tricky question of the prayer of asking, and the teaching he gives is hard. He says that the only thing we should ask for is God himself, and that if we ask for anything else it shows that we love earthly things too much. I agree with him that some of our prayers are a bit off-beam; someone once said to me, 'I'm praying for a two-bedroomed semi in the North of England, with a garden!' I can't cope with this at the same time as praying for refugees and homeless people. Yet I do think there are times when it is right for us to bring our needs and requests to God, as children come to a loving parent. Our needs and desires are, after all, an important part of our make-up, and it must be better to open them up to God, for him to deal with as he wills, rather than to repress them. I think Augustine would agree, because he says in a commentary on Psalm 66:2 (not included in this volume) that it is all right to pray for reasonable things like good health, but not a good idea to ask God for the death of a rich relation who will leave you pots of money.

What, then, are we to make of his teaching here? I think that Augustine is doing what Julian of Norwich also does, rather more gently: they point us to the centre of all prayer, from which all else follows. First and foremost we need simply to reach out to God, in and for himself. Julian prays in her *Revelations of the Divine Love:*

God of thy goodness, give me thyself;
for thou art enough for me,
and I can ask nothing that is less
that can be full honour to thee.
And if I ask anything that is less,
ever shall I be in want,
for only in thee have I all.'[1]

[1] From the translation by Fr John-Julian OJN, *A Lesson of Love*, DLT 1988, Chapter 5.

Both Julian and Augustine have glimpsed the freedom that comes when, beneath our surface longings, we desire God for his own sake, rather than for the things he might give us.

On the prayer of confession Augustine is uncompromising. 'Why flee from God?' he asks. 'You should rather run towards him.' *(God our judge, p. 84)*. In this powerful section he gives us a splendidly vivid picture of someone trying to escape from God: 'When you are planning some wrong-doing, you return home from the public arena so that none of your enemies may see, and you desert the common rooms of your home for the privacy of your bedroom. Even there, you are afraid there may be an intruder who will find you out, so you withdraw into your own heart and there ponder your wicked plans. But God is deeper within you than your own heart. Wherever you run to, he is there.'

I don't suppose that many readers of this book are about to try and hide from God in the broom-cupboard in order to plan a bank robbery. But it is good to remember that we can never avoid the presence and gaze of God, and that most of us do, at times, secretly work out how to score a point against those who have hurt us, or invent little untruths to cover up our mistakes, or find reasons to justify passing on juicy bits of gossip. In these murky corners of our hearts we cannot escape from our all-seeing God. 'So,' says Augustine, 'we must now come before him in confession. He whom you have angered will receive you with gentleness.' Who says that Augustine only knew the tough side of God?

It may seem to the reader that Augustine is so full of words and concepts that he doesn't give much space for stillness and awe in God's presence. But his writings do sometimes move from theological reflection into prayer where words are clearly inadequate. I remember as a theology student beavering away on an essay about Augustine's teaching on the Trinity. I had worked through the series of models that he uses to try and convey how God can be both Three and One (based on the human memory, understanding and will), and I was feeling that this was all rather dry and intellectual. Suddenly I came to this wonderful passage in Book 15 of his *De Trinitate*:

'I dare not claim to have said anything worthy of the unspeakable greatness of the supreme Trinity, whom I have not yet the strength to contemplate with unwavering eyes . . . The reader, upon the remembering, beholding and loving of that supreme Trinity, may recall it, contemplate it, delight in it, and make all his life depend on it . . . So were it better to bring this book at last to an end, not with argument but with prayer.' As I read this I found myself taken up, with Augustine, into a sense of wonder which was beyond words.

One passage in the present selection gives us a hint of the same mystery. In *Praise God even in sleep* (p. 105), Augustine writes: 'We began to speak the blessing, "Bless the Lord, my soul" . . . we sang until we had sung enough, *and then we fell silent*, but should we therefore have

ceased from blessing God in the inmost part of our being?'
(my italics). All words, and especially words of prayer and
worship, point beyond themselves. I like to think that my
prayers deepen in the silence that follows my words, and
that some of that stillness continues to flow beneath all my
activities – even to the point where, as Augustine playfully
suggests, I can praise God while I am asleep!

As has been said, Augustine is sometimes described as a
world-hater. He does talk about sex in mostly negative
terms, because his own conversion had centred around
giving up his considerable sexual activity. But he is not
a puritan kill-joy. At times he positively enthuses over
creation: 'Is there not beauty in the earth, the sea, the
air, the sky and the stars, and are we not moved by awe
when we consider them?' (*The beauty of heaven,* p. 121).
(Yet he doesn't like creepy-crawlies: 'But here amidst this
almost unutterable beauty and loveliness there live among
you worms and mice and all the earth's creeping vermin.'
He thinks heaven will be better, because 'only the angels
will be living among us.' I can't help wondering what a
nasty shock Augustine may have had if he got to heaven
and found celestial caterpillars.)

His main concern is to lead us from appreciating the
world's beauty to praising God himself: 'God's unseen
characteristics may be grasped through the visible things
which he has made. Wonder at it, and seek its Creator,'
(*Seeing God the inexpressible,* p. 102). It is from this
starting point, rather than a world-hating one, that
Augustine warns against worldliness. He is only cautious

about scientific research because he fears that some scientists may not have a sense of reverence, or be aware of the moral issues involved. In the passage quoted above, he goes on to tell a fantastic parable of greed, to show us how the desire for material things can lead to insatiable ambition, and how self-indulgence can never lead to happiness: 'If you love to possess things, then you will desire the whole earth, so that all who are born in it shall be your vassals and your slaves. And when the whole of the earth is yours, what then? You will ask for the sea in which you cannot live. The fish shall outdo you in this kind of greed. But perhaps the islands may be yours. Do not rest content with them, ask for the air . . . Let your desire reach even to the stars; say that the sun is yours . . .' *(Nothing more beautiful than God*, p. 41–2). Then comes the punch line: 'But you will find nothing more precious, nothing more sweet than he himself who made all things.' St Francis of Assisi, that great lover of God and of creation, would have agreed.

All this is quite different from the chilly and soul-destroying brand of self-denial that torments Maggie Tulliver in George Eliot's novel *The Mill on the Floss*. In this story, Maggie gets hold of a copy of *The Imitation of Christ* by Thomas à Kempis, and takes to heart his words about the danger of 'enjoying our own will and pleasure'. She then comes to the passage: 'Thou must set out courageously and lay the axe to the root, that thou mayst pluck up and destroy that hidden inclination to thyself, and unto all private and earthly good . . . Forsake thyself, resign thyself.' Her response to this is to make numerous plans of 'self-humiliation' and 'renunciation'. From then on she refuses to look at herself in the mirror, lies on the hard floor at night, denies herself books and music – which she loves – except the church organ and holy literature, and tells the lad who loves her, 'I wish we could have been friends . . . But that is the trial I have to bear in everything . . . I must part with everything I cared for when I was a child. And I must part with you.' As she speaks her eyes fill with tears.[1]

Such a blind and rigid asceticism is not what Augustine intends for his readers. He wants us to look at our priorities, and stresses that the good things of this world point to God, and are not to be grasped for our own selfish ends. In some passages he does seem to want to make us uncomfortable if we have any money in the bank: 'True Christians should not be rich, but should recognize that they really are poor,' he thunders (*Poverty of spirit,* p. 110). But his real concern is to encourage us to be poor in spirit, sharing our material goods, and knowing that we are empty inside, and need to be filled with God's grace: 'Why, unlike the rich, are the poor satisfied? What is this satisfaction, and where does it come from? It is from God, for God himself is the bread which is given,' (*God is our bread,* p. 118).

Augustine was influenced by certain individuals living a life of prayer and self-denial in the deserts of Egypt and Syria. These men and women had left the civilization of

[1] *The Mill on the Floss,* George Eliot, Pan, 1973 edition, from pages 271 and 284.

towns and villages in order to live in extreme simplicity. They wanted to be utterly free to listen to God and live for him alone, and their story was part of the inspiration behind Augustine's own rule for his monastic community at Thagaste. Here he laid down a frugal and self-disciplined life, but warned against self-inflicted punishments that would make people ill or suppress all natural feelings. His asceticism was not inhuman.

Augustine may have lived in a different world from ours, but he was as familiar as we are with violence and conflict, rampant selfishness and the abuse of material things. As barbarian tribes swept through the former Roman Empire it must have been hard to hang on to any hope in ultimate goodness, as it is for us when broadcasts and newspapers bring us face to face with human cruelty and mass starvation. From the moment Rome fell, Augustine began to teach that Christians are members of the only city that is truly secure, the 'City of God'. He therefore pinned a lot of hope on the final righting of all wrongs at the last times. This was not pious escapism from the hard realities of life, so much as an expression of the gospel: Christ's victory over sin and evil on the cross affects us in all time and beyond time. So Augustine is trying to help us to face the horror and darkness of our world, by putting it into a context of ultimate hope. He does this in a passage that must have been inspired by the vision of a new heaven and a new earth in Revelation 21: 'And God shall not turn his face away from us, for we shall see him as he is. And we shall not be poor, for God himself will be all in all . . . And when we are raised up, we shall not be upset and brought low, for there will be no adversity, and we shall not face God's anger even for a moment, for we shall abide in his loving kindness' (*Prudent fear and patience,* pp. 93–4).

When hatred seems unending in Northern Ireland, and brutality continues in Somalia and the former Jugoslavia; when a frail Pakistani pensioner is killed by a young white man in my own city as he walks to the mosque; and when there is so much crime, poverty and unemployment, passages such as this help me to hang on by my fingertips to my trust in God's ultimate goodness to a world gone mad.

A good place to end this introduction is with Augustine's thoughts on the 'good shepherd'. In *You seek but you are sought* (page 78), he reflects on some special aspects of the parable: 'The sheep did not seek the shepherd until it had left the flock and the shepherd came in search of it . . . So begin to seek him now, who first sought you, and carried you back on his shoulders.' This is a lovely reminder that Jesus, our Shepherd, was seeking us, his lost and wayward sheep, before it had even occurred to us to look for him. Augustine goes on to show that if Christ sought us and tenderly put us on his shoulder *even when we were not seeking him,* how much more will he be our shepherd, guide and helper now that we are trying to seek him in our lives.

Augustine knew from his own experience that, however messy and mixed up our inner life may be, we have a Lord who is constantly and tenderly seeking us. We never stop needing God, and he reaches out to us in his mercy, no matter how low we have fallen. An Anglican bishop of our own day has neatly summed this up: "We're not up to it, but God is down to it!"[1] But the final word must be with Augustine himself, in a great outpouring of relief and thankfulness:

'"O Lord open my lips and I shall give you praise." "Give you praise" because I have been created. "Give you praise" because, though I have sinned, you have not abandoned me. "Give you praise" because you have prompted me to confess my sins. "Give you praise" because I have been cleansed in order that I might be saved. "O Lord open my lips and I shall give you praise,"' (*Praise of God*, p. 69).

*Angela Ashwin*

[1] Bishop David Jenkins, from a sermon delivered in Sunderland in May 1993.

# Augustine of Hippo:
# His Life and Works

The man we remember as Augustine, Bishop of Hippo, was one of the great figures of the early Church. Born in 354 at Thagaste in modern-day Numidia, he studied and taught in Africa before moving to Rome and to Milan, where he reached the height of his career as a teacher of rhetoric and grammar. Augustine was a master of Latin literature and style, and was also closely in touch with the religious trends of his age. As a young man, he became interested in the Manichaean religion which, with its appeal to myth and dualistic understanding of the world, offered rather simplistic answers to complex questions. Later he discovered in the writings of the Platonists a sophisticated spiritual philosophy which stressed the importance of the immaterial mind. It was under the influence of Ambrose at Milan, however, that Augustine moved back to the Catholic Christianity of his mother, who all her life had prayed for his conversion.

In practical terms, conversion for Augustine meant embracing celibacy and renouncing his highly successful career. Following his painful decision to adopt a new life-style and to accept baptism (in 387), which he records in his *Confessions*, Augustine threw himself into Christianity with remarkable vigour. Over the next few years he began the vast outpouring of theological writing that was to exercise such an influence upon the Western Church, as well as committing himself to a monastic way of life and being ordained as priest. In 395 (or 396), he was ordained Bishop and moved to Hippo, where he founded about himself a community of like-minded clerics.

During his remaining years, until his death in 430, Augustine travelled, preached and taught as well as producing great works of theology in which, often in response to divergent forms of Christian belief, he was able to develop his distinctive understanding of the Christian revelation. In *The City of God*, for instance, Augustine developed his idea of the Church in the world and in human history, in *On the Trinity* he wrote of the human soul as image of God and, in his anti-Donatist and anti-Pelagian writings, he elaborated his doctrine of the sacraments and divine grace respectively.

Augustine's writings include works which are autobiographical, doctrinal, philosophical and apologetic, as well as sermons and extensive commentaries on Scripture. From this great mass of material the present anthology is based upon just one work: his *Exposition of the Psalms*. And yet, in some ways, this is the richest of all Augustine's books; it is certainly the longest. In fact, Augustine wrote it over a period of some twenty-four years, from 392 until 416 (or 422), and he included in it all the deepest elements of his thought and experience. In these pages we see him reflecting upon the mystery of the Church, as Christ on earth, upon the enigma of suffering, death and the after-life, upon the unfathomable movements of grace within the human spirit that makes us beautiful with the 'beauty of God'. Above all, the *Exposition of the Psalms* is a profoundly mystical work which is rooted in the discovery of the manifold presence of Christ at the centre of all our life and experience. The present selection represents only a small part of the wealth which this book contains; but we hope that it will be enough for the reader to share in the breadth and depth of Augustine's Christian vision.

*Oliver Davies*

# Short Bibliography

**Text:**
Corpus Christianorum, Series Latina, Turnhout and Paris, *Ennarationes in Psalmos*, 39, 40 and 41.

**Translations:**
*Expositions on the Book of Psalms*, ed. Philip Schaff, The Nicene and Post-Nicene Fathers of the Christian Church, First Series, 8 (repr. Eerdmans, 1983).
*St Augustine on the Psalms*, transl. Scholastica Hebgin and Felicitas Corrigan, Ancient Christian Writers 29, Westminster: Newman, 1960.

**Studies:**
*Augustine of Hippo*, Peter Brown, Faber and Faber, 1967.
*Augustine*, Henry Chadwick, Oxford University Press, 1986.

# SELECTIONS FROM EXPOSITION OF THE PSALMS

# An image of the Church

I remember that I promised to consider in this psalm how the moon is an apt symbol of the Church. There are two credible theories concerning the moon and I consider it to be either impossible or difficult for us to know which of them is the true one.

For when we enquire about the source of the moon's light, then some people answer that it produces it itself, that half of its globe is bright and half is dark and that, as it revolves in its orbit, it slowly turns the bright part towards the earth and into our sight, and so it appears to us at first to be horned . . . According to this theory, the moon represents the Church because the Church shines in its spiritual part, while in its carnal part it is dark. Sometimes the spiritual part becomes visible in good works but sometimes it lies hidden in the conscience and is known to God alone . . .

Others, however, say that the moon does not produce its own light but is illumined by the sun . . . According to this view too, the moon represents the Church, which does not possess its own light but is illumined by the only begotten Son of God, who is allegorically called a 'sun' in many parts of Holy Scripture. Certain heretics, through their ignorance of him and inability to perceive him, seek to turn the minds of simple people away from him and towards that physical and visible sun which is the light common to humanity and flies. And they do draw some people away, who for as long as they fail to gaze with their minds upon the interior light of truth, refuse to be content with the Catholic faith in its simplicity, which is the sole security for babes and by which milk alone they can arrive in certain health at the firm support of more solid food.

And so whichever of these two opinions is true, the moon is an apt allegorical image for the Church. But even if we lack the time and the interest to exercise our mind in such difficult matters, which are more troublesome than useful, or even if the mind itself is not capable of understanding them, then it is enough to look at the moon with our ordinary eyes. We do not have to seek out obscure causes but only observe how the moon waxes, is full and wanes. And if it wanes to nothing in order to be renewed, then even to the unlearned the moon represents the Church, in which we hold a belief in the resurrection of the dead.

*(11)*

# Purification through suffering

'The eyes of the Lord are toward the righteous . . .' So do not be afraid, but work; the eyes of the Lord rest upon you. '. . . and his ears toward their cry.' What more do you want? If the head of the family in a large household did not listen to his servant's grievances, then the servant would complain and say: 'How much we are suffering and no one hears us!' But can you say that of God: 'How much I am suffering and no one hears me!'?

Perhaps you say: 'If he heard me, then he would free me from my troubles; I call out to him and still I am afflicted'. If only you keep to his ways, then he will hear you when you are in distress.

But he is a surgeon, and there is still something rotten in you. You cry out, but still he cuts and will not remove his hand until he has cut away as much as seems right. Indeed, the cruel surgeon is the one who hears a man and spares his wound and corruption. Don't mothers rub their children in the bath for their health? And don't the children cry out at their hands? And are they then cruel in not hearing and sparing the tears? Aren't these women full of affection? Still the children cry out, and they are not spared. And our God, too, is full of love and, therefore, seems not to hear so that he can heal and spare us for all eternity.

*(34)*

39

# Release from suffering

'The Lord is near to the broken hearted, and saves the crushed in spirit.' If God is exalted, then the Christian must be lowly. If he wants the high God to draw near to him, then he must be humble. This is a great mystery, brothers and sisters. God is above all things; if you elevate yourself, then you will not touch him, but if you humble yourself, then he will descend to you.

'Many are the afflictions of the righteous.' Does he say: 'Therefore let Christians be righteous, let them hear my word so that they will no longer be afflicted'? He does not promise this, but says: 'Many are the afflictions of the righteous'. Rather, if they are sinful, then they shall have fewer troubles; if they are righteous, they shall have many.

Yet after the former have had few troubles or none, they shall come into eternal affliction, from which there shall be no escape; while the just shall have eternal peace after much tribulation, where they shall suffer no evil. 'Many are the afflictions of the righteous; but the Lord delivers him out of them all.'

(34)

# *Nothing more beautiful than God*

'Then my soul shall rejoice in the Lord . . .', that is, 'rejoice' in him who said: 'I am your salvation', not seeking other riches from without, not seeking to have many pleasures and the good things of the earth, but freely loving the true Spouse, not wishing to receive from him what gives delight, but wanting only to have him who is the source of all delight. For what can I be given that is better than God alone?

God loves me; and God loves you. So he has declared to you: ask for what you want. If a king said to you: ask for what you want, what honours and dignities you would come out with! What great things you would imagine both to receive and to give away to others. When God says to you: ask for what you want, then what will you ask for? Search your mind, exercise your avarice, reach out as far as you can and increase your desire. It is not just anyone, but it is the omnipotent God who says: ask for what you want.

If you love to possess things, then you will desire the whole earth, so that all who are born in it shall be your vassals and your slaves. And when the whole of the earth is yours, what then? You will ask for the sea in which you cannot live. The fish shall outdo you in this kind of greed. But perhaps the islands may be yours. Do not rest content with them, ask for the air, even though you cannot fly. Let your desire reach even to the stars; say that the sun is yours, the moon, the stars, because he who made all things says: ask for what you want. But you will find nothing more precious, nothing more sweet than he himself who made all things.

If you ask for him who made everything, then in him and from him you will have all the things which he has made. All things are precious, because all things are beautiful, but what is more beautiful than him? Many things are strong, but what is stronger than him? And he desires to give nothing more than himself. If you find anything that is better than him, then ask for it. If you ask for anything else, then you will do him wrong and yourself harm by preferring to him that which he made, when he who made these things would give himself to you.

(35)

# *All of life is worship*

'Let those who desire my vindication shout for joy and be glad and say evermore, "Great is the Lord, who delights in the welfare of his servant!" Then my tongue shall tell of thy righteousness and of thy praise all the day long'. But whose tongue can praise God all the day long? And now I have allowed this talk to go on a little longer, and you are tired. Who can praise God all the day long? I will suggest a remedy whereby you can praise God all day if you so wish.

Whatever it is that you do, do it well, and you will have praised God.

When you sing a hymn, you praise God; but what can your tongue achieve unless your heart also praises him? When you stop singing the hymn, and go away in order to take some refreshment, then you will praise God if you do not have too much to drink. If you leave in order to sleep, then you will praise God if you do not get up in the morning to do evil things. Are you involved in business? Then do not deceive anyone, and you will have praised God. Do you labour in the fields? Then do not stir up trouble. It is by the innocence of what you do that you can train yourself to praise God all the day long.

(35)

# The spring and the light

From what spring shall you drink, and from where does the torrent of God's desire flow? 'For with you', he says, 'is the spring of life.' Who is the spring of life if not Christ? He came to you in the flesh, so that he could quench your great thirst; he will satisfy you if you hope, as he did when you were thirsty. 'For with you is the spring of life; in your light do we see light.'

Here on earth a spring is one thing and light another; but not so in heaven. The spring and the light are one, and you can call it whatever you want, since in itself it is not the words you use for it and you cannot find a suitable name for it. One name cannot contain it. If you say that it is light only, someone will tell you: then why have I been told to hunger and thirst, for who can eat light? It has been said to me clearly: 'Blessed are the pure in heart for they shall see God'. If it is light, then I must prepare my eyes. But prepare your lips too, because that which is light is also a spring: a spring because it satisfies the thirsty, light because it enlightens the blind. In this life light is sometimes in one place, and a spring in another. For sometimes springs flow in darkness and sometimes in a desert you will suffer from the sun without finding a spring.

On earth these two things can be separated, but in heaven you will not thirst, for there is a stream, nor will you wander in darkness, for there is light.          *(36)*

# Welcoming the will of God

'O continue thy steadfast love to those who know you, and your salvation to the upright of heart.' As I have frequently said, in order to have an upright heart we need to follow the will of God in this life. Sometimes it is God's will that you should be in good health, and sometimes it is that you should suffer illness. And if God's will is sweet to you when you are in health, and bitter when you are ill, then you do not have an upright heart. Why is this so? Because you do not want to conform your will to the will of God, but you want to bend his will to yours. But his will is true while yours is crooked; and it is right to conform your will to his, rather than his to yours. Then you will have an upright heart.

If things go well for you in this world, let God be praised, who comforts you, and if things are difficult, let God be praised, who tries you and purifies you. In this way you will have an upright heart, saying: 'I will bless the Lord at all times; his praise shall ever be in my mouth'.

(36)

# The life to come

This is what disturbs you as a Christian, the fact that you see those who do evil leading contented lives, surrounded by an abundance of things like these: good health, distinguished honours, their family untouched by affliction, their relatives rejoicing, their dependants willing to please, their influence at its height, their life uninterrupted by any sad event. You see their immense resources and their moral bankruptcy, and you say in your heart that there is no divine judgement, that all things are governed by chance and are blown about at random. For if God, you say, were really concerned with human affairs, would that person's evil flourish and my innocence suffer?

Now there is a remedy to be found in Holy Scripture for every kind of spiritual disease. Whoever is ill in this way, and feels such things in their heart, should drink deep for this psalm . . .

'Fret not yourself because of the wicked, be not envious of wrongdoers. For they will soon fade like the grass, and wither like the green herb.' What still seems a long way off for you is 'soon' in the sight of God. Yield to God, and it will become 'soon' for you too. What he calls 'grass' is what we understand to be 'green herb'. These are worthless things that have only a tenuous hold on the ground for they lack deep roots. And so in the winter they are green, but when the summer sun begins to burn, they wither away. Now is the time of winter, and your glory is not yet visible. But if your love has roots that are deep, as do many trees in the winter, then the cold will pass, and summer will come, which is the day of judgement. Then the green grass will fade and the glory of the trees will appear. 'For you have died', the apostle says, just as trees in the winter seem to be withered and dead. And what is our hope if we are dead? The root is within, and where our root is, there too is our life and there our love: '. . . and your life is hid with Christ in God.'

When shall they wither who have such a root? When will our spring come? When our summer? When shall we be clothed with the honour of leaves and enriched with an abundance of fruit? When shall this be? Hear what follows: 'When Christ who is our life shall appear, then you too shall appear with him in glory'.

(37)

# The vision of God

'And their heritage will abide for ever.' We hold this by faith; but does the Lord too know it by faith? The Lord knows these things more clearly than we could say, even when we will have been made equal to the angels. For those things which shall be made plain shall not be as plain to us as they are now to him, in whom there is no change.

And yet what is said even of us? 'Beloved, we are God's children now; it does not yet appear what we shall be, but we know that when he appears we shall be like him, for we shall see him as he is.' Therefore some kind of blissful vision awaits us which, although it can be perceived in some measure now as 'in a mirror dimly', is a ravishing beauty of bliss that can in no way be spoken of, which God reserves for those who fear him and which he brings to perfection in those who hope in him. It is for this that our hearts are being prepared in all the troubles and temptations of this present life.

And do not be surprised that you are prepared for it by suffering, for you are being prepared for something that is great. This is why we hear the words of the righteous man: 'I consider that the sufferings of this present time are not worth comparing with the glory that is to be revealed to us'.

And what will our future glory be but that we are made equal to the angels and shall see God? How great a gift he gives to the blind man whose eyes he heals so that they can see this light? . . . How can we repay the One who heals us by cleansing our interior eyes so that they can see this eternal light which is God himself?

(37)

# The poverty of God

'For those blessed by the Lord shall possess the land', just as they shall possess the Righteous One, he who alone is both himself truly righteous and makes us righteous, he who was both a poor man in this world and who brought great riches to it with which to make rich those whom he had found poor.

For it is he who made the hearts of the poor rich with the Holy Spirit and, having emptied their souls by the confession of sins, filled them with all the wealth of righteousness. He who was able to make the fisherman rich who, by leaving his nets, disregarded what he already had and drew up what he did not yet have.

For God chose the weak things of the world to confound the strong. So it was not by the orator that he won for himself the fisherman, but by the fisherman that he won the orator, by the fisherman that he won the senator and by the fisherman that he won the emperor.

(37)

# The sufferings of the just

'For the Lord loves justice; he will not forsake his saints.'
When the saints experience suffering, we should not
think that God does not judge, or that he does not do
so justly. Will he who warns us to judge justly, himself
judge unjustly? 'For the Lord loves justice; he will not
forsake his saints.' But consider how the life of the saints
is 'hid with him', so that those who suffer now on earth
are like trees lacking fruit and foliage during the time
of winter. Consider how, when their Saviour appears
like a newly-risen sun, the life in their roots shall be
manifest in their fruit. He does indeed then love 'justice',
and 'he will not forsake his saints'.

(37)

# The end of time

'Make haste to help me, O Lord, my salvation!' This is that very salvation, brothers and sisters, concerning which, as the apostle Peter says, the prophets searched and inquired, though they did not find what they sought. But they inquired into it and foretold it, while we have come and found what they searched for. Although, at the same time, we ourselves have not yet received it. What is more, others after us shall be born and shall find what they themselves do not receive, and will pass away.

And so at the end of the day we shall all receive the 'penny of salvation' together, in the company of the patriarchs and the prophets and the apostles. For you know that the hired labourers were taken to the vineyard at different times, and yet they all received equal wages. And so the prophets and apostles and martyrs and ourselves, and those who come after us until the end of time, shall receive the same eternal salvation at the conclusion of all things. Thus, contemplating the glory of God and beholding his face, we shall praise him in eternity, free from imperfection, free from any punishments of wrong-doing, free from any perversity of sin, praising him, and not longing for him any more but now possessing him, for whom we longed to the very end, and in whom we rejoiced in hope.

For we shall be in that city, where God is our good, where God is our light, our bread and our life. We shall find in him whatever good thing there is, whose absence now causes us grief. In him there will be that peace which, when we think of it now, causes us to suffer and to be filled with longing. For we remember that 'day of rest' in the recollection of which we have said so much already, and so much needs to be said ceaselessly — not with the lips but with the heart, for with our lips we are silent that our hearts may cry out.

*(38)*

# *Unceasing prayer*

'Lord, all my longing is know to you.' It is not known to other people who cannot see the heart, but 'all my longing is known to you'. Let your longing be known to him, our Father, and he, who sees hidden things, will reward you. For it is your heart's desire that is your prayer, and if your desire endures, then your prayer too shall endure. It was with good reason that the apostle said: 'Pray without ceasing'.

Are we then to kneel, to bow low and to lift our hands continuously, as he says: 'Pray without ceasing'? If we say that this is our prayer, then I do not think that we shall be able to do it ceaselessly. But there is another kind of interior prayer, which is the desire of the heart. And so if, whatever else you may do, you long for the Sabbath, then your prayer will have no end.

If you wish to pray without end, then keep the desire of your heart alive. The continuation of your longing is the continuation of your prayer. If you no longer love, then your prayer, too, will end.

Who are those whose prayer has fallen silent? Concerning these it is said: 'Because wickedness is multiplied, most men's love will grow cold' [Matt.24:12]. The growing cold of love is the silence of the heart; the burning of love is the heart's cry. If love always remains, your heart will always cry out. If you always cry out, you will always feel longing, and if you feel longing, you will always remember the Sabbath rest.

*(38)*

# The uncertainty of life

'Surely for naught are they in turmoil.' The psalmist returns to what he mentioned a short while ago. So, although he is making progress here, he says, 'surely for naught are they in turmoil', inasmuch as he still lives in a state of uncertainty.

For who is sure even of their own goodness? 'For naught are they in turmoil.' Let them cast their cares upon the Lord; let their cast upon him whatever is the source of their anxiety.

Let God nurture you, let him keep you.

For are we certain of anything in this life but death? Even when we consider together all the good things and all the evil things of this life, all those belonging to justice and all those to iniquity, what is there that is certain here but death?

You have made some progress, yet all you know is what you are today; what you shall be tomorrow, you do not know. You are a sinner, yet all you know is what you are today; what you shall be tomorrow, you do not know. And you live in hope of wealth, but it is uncertain whether you will have it. You hope for a wife, but it is uncertain whether you will find her, or what kind of wife you will find. You hope for sons, but it is uncertain whether they shall be born. And if they have been born, it is uncertain whether they will live. If they live, it is uncertain whether they will grow in virtue or whether they will turn out badly. Whichever direction you turn, all things are uncertain. Death alone is sure.

If you are poor, it is uncertain whether you will become rich; if you are unlearned, it is uncertain whether you will be educated; if you are ill, it is uncertain whether you will recover. But if you have been born, it is certain that you will die. And even though the fact of your dying is certain, the day of your death is uncertain. And so among all these uncertainties, in the midst of which only death is certain (though when it will happen is not) and only death is greatly guarded against (though it cannot be escaped), it is clear that 'all living people are troubled in vain'.

(39)

# God is more beautiful

'Blessed is the one who makes the Lord his trust, who does not turn to the proud, or to those who go astray after false gods!' See the way you wanted to go; see the great crowd who follow the wide path. It is not without reason that that road leads to the amphitheatre, and it is not without reason it leads to death. The broad way brings death; its breadth delights for a while, but its end is narrow for all eternity.

The crowd make great noise as they hurry on, they rejoice as they flock together. Do not imitate them, do not turn aside after them, for they are 'proud' and 'after false gods'.

Let the Lord your God be your hope. Hope for nothing else from the Lord your God, but let your Lord himself be your hope.

For there are many who hope that our Lord will make them wealthy, or will get them short-lived honours, and they hope for everything else from God except God himself.

But you should seek your God himself. Indeed, despising all other things, hasten to him. Forgetting all other things, be mindful of him. Leaving all other things behind, reach out towards him. For certainly he it was who put you right when you were on the wrong path, and now that you are on the right path, he it is who guides you and leads you on. And so he should be your hope who leads you and guides you.

To what end does worldly avarice lead you and guide you? First you desired a farm, then you wanted to have an estate and to keep your neighbours out. Then, having shut them out, you desired the lands of other neighbours. You extended your desires until you reached the shores of the sea and, upon arriving at the shores, you desire the islands and, when you possess the whole earth, you would then want the heavens.

Leave all your loves; he is more beautiful who made heaven and earth.

(40)

# On humility of spirit

'My soul is cast down within me.' Am I depressed because of God, or because of myself?

My soul is renewed by him who knows no change, but it is distressed by what is always subject to change. I know that the righteousness of God endures, but I do not know whether my own righteousness will endure. And so I am alarmed when the apostle says: 'Therefore let anyone who thinks that he stands take heed lest he fall' [1 Cor. 10:12]. And since there is no solidity in me, and I have no hope in myself: 'My soul is cast down within me'.

Do you wish to be free from your depression? Then do not remain in yourself, but say: 'To you, O Lord, I have lifted up my soul'. In other words: do not place your hope in yourself but in your God. For if you hope in yourself, then you will be the cause of your soul's depression, for you will find nothing certain within yourself. And so since I am the cause of my own depression, what remains but humility, so that the mind does not presume too much of itself? What remains but to make ourselves the smallest thing of all, to humble ourselves, so that we shall deserve to be raised on high? Humility grants nothing to itself, so that it shall be granted what is precious to it.

*(42)*

# God comes to our aid in times of trouble

'By day the lord commands his steadfast love; and at night his song is with me.' No one has time to listen when they are beset by troubles. And so pay heed when things go well with you; listen when things go well with you; learn, when you have peace, the discipline of wisdom and store up the word of God as your food. For in time of trouble we must all profit from what we heard when we were secure . . .

And when troubles come, he will not withhold his help. He will show you that what he commands by day is true. For somewhere it is written: 'The mercy of the Lord is seasonable in the time of affliction, as clouds of rain in the time of drought'.

'By day the Lord commands his steadfast love; and at night his song is with me.' He does not show you that he is your support until troubles come from which you must be saved by him who gave you his promise 'by day'. And so we are urged to be like the ant. For just as 'day' symbolizes worldly prosperity, and 'night' the times of trouble, so too do 'summer' and 'winter'. And what do the ants do? They store up in the summer what they will need in the winter. So while the summer lasts, while things go well with you and you live in peace, listen to the word of the Lord. For how could you possibly cross the whole of the sea without difficulty, with all the storms of this world? How could that be? Who has ever had that good fortune? And even if they did, then the calm would be all the more ominous. 'By day the Lord commands his steadfast love; and at night his song is with me.'

*(42)*

# The sacrifice within

'A prayer to the God of my life.' This is what I shall do in this life, I who am a 'hart that thirsts and longs for running streams', recalling the sweetness of that voice by which I was led through the tabernacle to the house of God. While this corruptible body presses down the soul, I shall make 'a prayer to the God of my life'.

For in order to worship my God, I do not have to buy anything from across the seas nor, in order that he should hear me, do I have to sail far away to get incense and perfumes, nor do I even have to bring from my flock a calf or a ram.

'A prayer to the God of my life.' The victim to sacrifice is within myself; the incense to place upon the altar is within me; the sacrifice to offer to my God is within: 'the sacrifice acceptable to God is a broken spirit'.

(42)

# The one wisdom

What a nuptial song!

See, in the midst of the songs which are full of joy, the bride herself comes forth. For previously it was the bridegroom who was coming; it was he who was described and all our attention was focused on him. Now let the bride too come forth. 'At your right hand stands the queen in gold of Ophir.' She who sits on the left is no queen. For they will stand on the left to whom it will be said: 'Depart from me, you who are cursed, into the eternal fire'. But she will stand on the right to whom it will be said: 'Come, O blessed of my Father, inherit the kingdom prepared for you from the foundation of the world'.

'At your right hand stands the queen in gold of Ophir', and 'in many-coloured robes she is led to the king.' What are the robes of this queen? Both precious and varied, they are the mysteries of doctrine in all the different languages, whether African, Syrian, Greek, Hebrew or whatever. It is these languages which make the multi-coloured character of this queen's robes. But just as all the variety of her clothes blend into one harmony, thus all the languages are united in one faith. Let there be variety in her clothes, but no tear.

And if we have understood the variety of her clothes to be the diversity of languages, and her clothes to be the principle of unity, what then is the 'gold' within this diversity? It is wisdom itself. However great the variety of languages, there is only one gold which is proclaimed: not different kinds of gold, but the same gold in different forms. For it is the same wisdom, the same doctrine and discipline which is preached in all the different languages. There is diversity in the languages, but gold in what is said.

*(45)*

# The beauty of the bride

'Forget your people and your father's house; and the king will desire your beauty.' What is that but the beauty which is of his own making? He 'will desire your beauty' – whose beauty? The beauty of the sinful woman, wicked and ungodly, who was with her 'father', the devil, and among her own 'people'? No, but that of the woman of whom it is said: 'Who is it that comes up made white?' She was not white at first, but became white, for 'though your sins are as scarlet, they shall be as white as snow'.

'The king will desire your beauty' – what king is this? 'For he is the lord your God.' Now consider whether you should not leave your father and your people in order to come to this king, who is your God. He is your king and your God. He is your king and your spouse. You are joined in marriage to the king, your God, who provides your dowry, who adorns you, who redeems you, who makes you whole. Whatever there is in you that is pleasing to him, you have from him.

(45)

# Christic our life

'Like sheep they are appointed for Sheol; death shall be their shepherd.' Whose shepherd? Those whose way is a stumbling-block to themselves. Those who think only of the things that exist here and now, while for the future they have no concern. Those who think only of the life that must be called death. And so it is not without reason that they, like sheep in hell, have death as their shepherd.

What does this mean: to have death as a shepherd? For is death some thing or some power? The death which people fear is certainly the separation of the soul from the body, while true death, which people do not fear, is the separation of the soul from God. And very often when people fear that death which is the separation of the soul from the body, they fall victim to that death which is the separation of the soul from God. This, then, is death. But how is death 'their shepherd'? If Christ is life, the devil is death. It says in many parts of Scripture that Christ is life. And the devil is death, not because he is himself death, but because he is the cause of death . . . Those who belong to him have death as their shepherd, while we who have our minds fixed on the immortality to come and who bear the sign of the cross of Christ on our foreheads, have no shepherd but life. Death is the shepherd of the unbelievers, while the shepherd of those who have faith is life.

And so – are we already in heaven? We are in heaven by our faith. For if we are not in heaven, why is it said that we should 'lift up' our hearts? If we are not in heaven, then why does the apostle Paul say: 'Our conversation is in heaven'? In our bodies we walk on earth, while in our hearts we live in heaven. We live there if we send there anything that keeps us here. For no one lives anywhere with their heart, if that is not also where their thoughts are; but where our thoughts are, there our treasure is. If we lay up treasure on earth, then our heart will not leave the earth, but if we lay up treasure in heaven, our heart shall not leave heaven. For our Lord says plainly: 'Where your treasure is, there will your heart be also'.

*(49)*

# Praise of God

'O Lord, open my lips and I shall give you praise.' 'Give you praise' because I have been created. 'Give you praise' because, though I have sinned, you have not abandoned me. 'Give you praise' because you have prompted me to confess my sins. 'Give you praise' because I have been cleansed in order that I might be saved. 'O Lord open my lips and I shall give you praise.'

*(51)*

# Christ awake in you

'I would haste to find myself a shelter from the raging wind and tempest.' At times, there is the sea and the storm, and there is nothing you can do but cry out: 'Lord, I perish'. Then let him who steps without fear upon the waves stretch out his hand. Let him remove your anxiety and confirm his strength in you. Let him speak to you within and say to you: 'Turn your mind to me, and to what I have suffered. Perhaps it is an evil brother who is causing you grief, or a hostile stranger; but which of these have I not suffered?'

Though the storm rages, he saves us from weakness of mind and from the storm. Perhaps your ship is tossed about because he is asleep within it. While the sea raged, and the boat in which the disciples sailed was tossed about, Christ slept. Then finally they saw that among them was sleeping the ruler and creator of the winds, and so they approached Christ and roused him. He commanded the winds, and all became still. And so it is perhaps with good reason that your heart is disturbed, because you have forgotten him in whom you believe. You suffer beyond your endurance because you do not remember what Christ has done for you. And if you are not mindful of Christ, then he sleeps. Arouse Christ, and awake your faith.

For Christ slumbers in you if you do not recall his sufferings; but if you are mindful of his sufferings, then Christ is awake in you.

For when, with a whole heart, you have considered his sufferings, will you not then calmly endure what you suffer, even perhaps rejoicing that through your sufferings you bear a certain likeness to your King? So when you have begun to be comforted and to rejoice through thinking upon these things, he has then arisen, he has commanded the winds, and therefore there shall be a great calm. 'I would haste to find myself a shelter from the raging wind and tempest.'

(55)

# Building our house on rock

If we have been a little long-winded, then we ask your forgiveness. And we urge you in the name of Christ to think about what you have received and to benefit from it. For to preach the truth means nothing at all if the heart and the tongue are not in accord. And it means nothing for us to hear the truth if we do not build our house on rock. For that person builds on rock who both hears the Gospel and puts it into action, while they who hear but do not act, build on sand. And they who neither hear nor act, build nothing at all.

In the same way that they who build on sand construct their own ruin, those who do not build on rock will be caught without a home when the flood comes. There is nothing else for us to do but to build and to build on rock, which means to say: both to hear and to act . . .

And so when you have heard the Gospel, act upon it. For if you do not, then though you have built, you will have built on sand. If we are without a home, we are exposed, and if our home is built on sand, we shall be faced with ruin. And so we have no choice but to build our house on rock, by putting into action that which we have heard.

*(58)*

# The power of love

Let us appear to God in holy desire, so he may appear to us in the power and glory of his Son.

For there are many to whom he has not yet appeared. Let them also be filled with holy desire, so he may appear to them too.

And there are many who imagine him to be merely human, since it is said that he was born of a woman, that he was crucified, that he walked on the earth, that he ate and drank and did other things that mortals do. And they think he was just like other men. But you have heard in the Gospel how he also announced his immense majesty: 'I and the Father are one'. In becoming human, a majesty so great, such equality with the Father took flesh because of our weakness.

This is how we were loved by God, even before we ourselves loved him. And if, before we loved God, we were loved so much that he made his Son, his very equal, a human being for our sake, what does he reserve for us now that we love him?

Many people think it is insignificant that the Son of God should have appeared on earth. As they do not share in the Holy One, they do not see his power and his glory. That is, because their hearts are not yet made holy (which would give them the means to perceive the excellence of his virtue, and thank God that so great a One should come on their behalf, thanking him for so great a nativity, so great a Passion), they are blind to his glory and to his power.

*(63)*

# Trueness of heart

'Let the righteous rejoice in the Lord, and take refuge in him! Let all the upright in heart give glory!' For now the Lord has risen, now he has ascended to heaven, now he has shown that here is another life, now it is evident that his counsels, in which he lay concealed in the depth of your heart, were not empty, for his Blood was shed to be the price of the redeemed. Now all things are made clear, all things have been proclaimed and believed. And under the whole of heaven 'Let the righteous rejoice in the Lord, and take refuge in him! Let all the upright in heart give glory!'

But who are the upright in heart? Those who endure all things in this life, not attributing them to senseless chance, but to God's plan as medicine for us. Those who do not presume too much concerning their own righteousness, which makes them believe that their sufferings are unjust and that God is therefore unjust, because others who sin more do not suffer more . . .

God displeases you, but you are pleased with yourself, and so you have a crooked heart. And what is worse, you want to make God's heart crooked in accordance with your own, so that he does what you want, whereas you ought to do what he wishes you to do. What then? Do you wish to bend God's heart, which is always true, to match the depravity of your own? How much better it would be to correct your heart by his righteousness.

Is this not what your Lord has taught you, of whose Passion we were just speaking? Was he not bearing your weakness when he said: 'My soul is very sorrowful, even to death'? Did he not mean you in himself when he said: 'Father, if it be possible, let this cup pass from me'? For the Father and the Son do not have two hearts, one different from the other, but he bore your heart in the form of a servant, so that he might teach it by example. And see, tribulation has laid bare in you a second heart, as it were, which desired that what was about to happen should pass you by. But that is not what God wished. God does not consent to your heart; you should consent to his. Hear his voice, when he says: 'Nevertheless, not as I will, but as you will'.

*(64)*

# Examine your own heart

'If I had cherished iniquity in my heart, the Lord would not have listened.' Consider now, my brothers and sisters, how easily, even every day, people turn red and accuse others of sins. He does evil things, they say, he does base things, he is a wicked man; though perhaps it is fear of other people that leads us to say these things.

And so look to see whether you do not harbour wickedness in your own heart in case you should condemn in someone else what you yourself intend to do and, therefore, make a fuss about them, not because of what they do, but only because they have been found out.

Look within yourself. Be your own inner judge. In the secret chamber, in the innermost recess of your heart, where you are alone with him who sees all, there wickedness must be displeasing to you, so that you can be pleasing to God. Have no regard for it, then, nor love for it, but rather despise it, condemn it and turn away from it. Whatever pleasurable thing it has promised you in order to lead you to sin, whatever nasty thing it has threatened you with in order to drive you on to sin, it is all emptiness which passes away. Wickedness must be despised so that it can be trodden underfoot, and not dwelt on in case it should win us over.

(66)

# You seek but you are sought

'May all who seek you rejoice and be glad in you!' It is one thing to seek God and another to seek human beings. 'May all who seek you rejoice.' Those who seek themselves shall not rejoice, whom you, O Lord, sought before they sought you.

The sheep did not seek the shepherd until it had left the flock and the shepherd came in search of it. He sought it and carried it back on his shoulders. Will he, who first sought you, his sheep, when you spurned him and did not seek him, spurn you now that you seek him? And so begin to seek him now, who first sought you and carried you back on his shoulders. Do what he says: 'My sheep hear my voice, and I know them, and they follow me'.

If you seek him who first sought you, and if you become his sheep, and if you listen to the voice of your shepherd and follow him, then see what he will reveal to you of himself, of his body, in order that you should not err about him or the Church, for instance, when people claim that that man is Christ who is not Christ or that that is the Church which is not the Church. For there are many who say that Christ did not have a body and that Christ did not rise in his body. Do not follow such voices. Listen to the voice of your shepherd, who was clothed in flesh in order that he might seek lost flesh. He rose from the dead and said: 'Handle me, and see; for a spirit has not flesh and bones as you see that I have'. He shows himself to you; follow his voice. He shows you the Church, in case anyone should deceive you by the name of Church. He says: 'Thus it is written that the Christ should suffer and on the third day rise from the dead, and that repentance and forgiveness of sins should be preached in his name to all nations, beginning from Jerusalem'.

Since you have the voice of your shepherd, do not follow the voices of strangers. And you shall not need to fear a thief, if you have followed your shepherd's voice.

*(70)*

# New creation in God

'O God, you have taught me from my youth.' What have you taught me? That I ought to remember only your justice. For when I consider my past life I see what was due to me, and what I received instead. Punishment was due, but grace was given. Hell was due, but eternal life was given.

'O God, you have taught me from my youth.' From the very beginning of my life in the faith in which you had renewed me, you taught me that there was nothing about my life that allowed me to claim anything you gave as being owed to me. For no one is converted to God except from the ways of evil. No one is redeemed except from captivity, and who can claim, moreover, that their imprisonment was unjust, when they had abandoned their leader and defected to join a traitor? God is the leader, and the traitor is the devil. God taught us his commands, and the devil tempted us to deceit. Why did we hear this prompting to deceit? Is the devil better than God? Is the one who failed you better than the one who made you? You believed the devil's promises, and discovered instead what punishment was threatened by God.

So now we are freed from our captivity, in hope though not yet to full effect, walking in faith though not yet in full vision, and so the psalmist says: 'God has taught me from my youth'. From my youth I have turned to you, and have been renewed by you. I was made by you, and then made a new creation. I was shaped by you, and then reformed. I learned that my merits counted for nothing, but that your grace came to me freely, so that I would think only of your justice and righteousness.

(71)

# God is always good

'How good God is to Israel.' That is, good to the upright of heart. But to the perverse he will appear perverse. And in another psalm it says: 'With the holy you will be holy, and with the innocent you will be innocent, and with the perverse you will be perverse'.

Perverse people think that others are being perverse. But God cannot really be like this, far from it: he is what he is. It is just as when the sun's rays are gentle on healthy and clear eyes but strike bloodshot eyes like sharp spears: in both cases the sun is the same, but the person looking at it is different. So when you begin to be perverse, and God appears perverse to you, it is you who have changed, not God. What good people experience as a joy will be the torments of punishment to you.

Recalling this, then, the psalmist says: 'How good God is to Israel, to those who are upright of heart'.

*(73)*

# God our judge

God is the judge of your iniquities. If he is God, he is present everywhere. Where can you hide from his gaze or talk out of his hearing? If God were to come from the east to judge, you could hide in the west, and say whatever you like against him. If he came from the west, you could hide in the east and speak there. If he came from the mountain wilderness to judge, you could go into the middle of the crowds where you could safely mutter to yourself. But he comes from no place in particular to judge, for he is everywhere both hidden away and present before all.

None can understand God, yet none can remain ignorant of him; so see what you are doing, speaking iniquities against him. The Scriptures say elsewhere: 'The spirit of the Lord has filled the earth, and the surrounds of the entire universe have knowledge of his voice. Therefore those who speak iniquity cannot hide'.

So do not imagine that God exists in space. He is with you whether you are doing right or wrong, and you cannot disguise what you are doing. He is good to the good, and bad to the bad, your helper if you are good, and an avenger against you if you are bad.

You have a judge in the secret place of your heart. When you are planning some wrong-doing, you return home from the public arena so that none of your enemies may see, and you desert the common rooms of your home for the privacy of your bedroom. Even there, you are afraid there may be an intruder who will find you out, so you withdraw into your own heart and there ponder your wicked plans. But God is deeper within you than your own heart. Wherever you run to, he is there. You cannot run from your own self. Wherever you go, your own self has to follow. So there is nowhere you can run to from an angry God except to a God appeased. There is nowhere else to go. Why flee from him? You should rather run towards him, and not speak evil against him.

The psalm says: 'He has meditated on evil in his bedchamber'. Why in his bedchamber? His bedchamber is his heart, as it says: 'Pay a sacrifice of justice and hope in the Lord'. But an earlier line runs: 'Speak in your heart, and show compassion in your bedchamber'. As often as you are tempted there, allow yourself to be pricked by the urge to confess.

Wherever you speak evil against the Lord, he will be there to judge you. Though he delays punishment, his judgement is delivered immediately. At this time he sees and understands the fault, and judges, but he waits to give punishment. That punishment will come when there appears the face of the man who on earth was mocked, judged, crucified, who himself had to stand before the judge. When he appears as judge in his turn, then you will be punished, if you have not turned on to the right path.

So what we must do now is come before him in confession. He whom you have angered will receive you with gentleness. 'He will not come from the mountain wildernesses, for God is the judge.' Nor does he come from east or west, for if he were to be found in any *place* he would not be God. Since this is no human judge but God himself, do not expect him to come in this dimension of space. But he will be present within you if only you follow the way of goodness, if you confess to him and call upon his name.

(75)

# Calling upon God

The psalm says: 'With my voice have I cried to the Lord'. But many people cry to the Lord for the acquisition of wealth and the avoidance of loss, for the safety of their property, for the stability of their homes, for temporal happiness, for worldly dignity, and finally, for health of the body, which is the patrimony of the poor.

But few people want the Lord himself. It is easier to want something from him. As if what the Lord gives could be more agreeable than the Lord himself!

So anyone who cries to the Lord for anything but the Lord himself has not yet transcended their love of earthly things. But the psalmist (who has transcended this) says: 'With my voice have I cried to the Lord'. And to make clear that he is crying for the Lord himself and not for anything else, he adds: 'And my voice goes up to God'. For when we cry to God for some other intention, our voice does not go up to God, but goes towards whatever it is we are really wanting.

Now the psalmist freely loved God, willingly sacrificed to him, and leaving behind the things of earth, he saw nothing else in the heights on which to pour out his spirit except God, from whom, through whom and in whom he had been created, and to whom he had turned, saying: 'My voice goes up to God'. What is the reason for this? See what follows: 'And he attends to my cry'. Indeed, God will listen to you when you are seeking him, and not using him as a way to obtain something else.

It is said of some people that 'They cried to the Lord, but he was not the one to make them safe, nor did he even hear them'. This is because their voice did not *really* go up to the Lord. Scripture says of such people in another place, 'They did not call upon the Lord'. They were crying to him, but 'They did not call upon the Lord.'

This is because they were not inviting the Lord into their hearts. They did not want to be a dwelling place for the Lord.

What then happened to them? 'They trembled with fear where no fear was.' They trembled at the loss of their present goods, since they had not filled themselves with the one on whom they did not really call. They did not love with that freedom which would have enabled them to say when all earthly goods were lost: 'As it has pleased the Lord, so it has been done. Blessed be the name of the Lord.'

*(77)*

# The true poor

This psalm is entitled 'For the Winepress'. Like grapes we are put under pressure, and we are crushed. The reason is this: our love has carried us into an involvement with secular, temporal and perishable concerns, and so we suffer torments, tribulation and abundance of temptation.

Now, we must seek that place of rest which is not to be found in this life or on this earth. As it is written, the Lord becomes a refuge for the poor, that is, those who are destitute, without resources, help, or anything on earth they can rely on. To such is God made present.

But even if people on this earth are rich in money, they can understand what Paul means when he says: 'Teach the rich of this world not to be arrogant, nor to trust in the uncertainties of wealth'. For the wealth that gives them such pleasure is a very uncertain thing, and even before they enter that winepress which is the service of God, they can see how their riches put them under pressure. They worry about how to look after their wealth and guard it and, if they gradually come to love it, this love brings forth more fear than fruit. Nothing is so unstable as a spinning object, and it is appropriate that coins are minted in a round shape so that they can spin.

Rich people of this kind are poor even in the midst of their possessions. But those who lack wealth and yet yearn after it are classed along with the reprobate rich, for God does not take account of the powers a person has, but of the state of their will and purpose.

The true poor are destitute of all earthly hope, for even if wealth is flowing all around them, they understand how uncertain it is. They turn to God with groaning, as they find nothing in this age they can delight in or that grips their desire. But they are held in the heavy winepress of trials and temptations, and they flow out from this as oil and wine, which signify good desires. Such people have already gone beyond their love for the earth, and now they cannot but desire God. For they come to love the One who made heaven and earth, but they are not yet joined with him: the satisfaction is delayed that the desire might grow. So their desire is increased until it meets its object. For it is no small thing that God is in the process of giving to them, nor is their training for it a small matter, because he is not giving them something he has made, but is giving them himself, who made all.

Strive then to possess God. Live long in desire for that gift which you will have for all eternity.

*(84)*

# The spiritual race

And so, beloved, let each of you dedicate and return to the Lord what you can and as far as you are able. Let none look back to take delight in their former life, or turn from straining ahead to look behind.

We must keep on running until we reach our goal, for we are running in our desires, not with our feet. None can claim to have reached the goal in this life. For who can match St Paul in virtue? And he said: 'Brethren, I do not think I have reached my goal except in one respect: I have forgotten what went before, and I am now straining ahead, making for the heavenly prize, which is the calling of God in Christ Jesus'.

When you see how Paul was still running the race, you cannot be under the impression that you have already reached the goal.

*(84)*

# Christ both creator and creature

God could give no greater gift to humanity than that he should set over us his Word, through whom he created everything, and should form human beings to be as limbs of the Word, so that the Word might be Son of God and Son of Man, one God with the Father, and one with us.

When we pray to God then, we do not exclude the Son. And when the Son prays in his human nature, he does not separate his head from the rest of him, but is the one saviour of his own body, our Lord Jesus Christ, Son of God, who prays for us and within us, and is also prayed to by us. He prays for us as our priest, in us as our head, and he is prayed to by us as our God. Let us acknowledge our voice in him and his voice in us.

And when, particularly in prophecy, something is said about our Lord Jesus Christ which seems to suggest a certain lowliness unworthy of God, let us not hesitate to attribute it to him who did not hesitate to join himself to us. The whole of creation serves him, because through him everything was made. On the one hand, we behold him divine and sublime, and hear: 'In the beginning was the Word, and the Word was with God, and the Word was God. He was with God in the beginning, everything was made through him, and without him was nothing made.' So we see the Son of God's divinity higher than any sublime creature within creation. Yet, on the other hand, we hear him elsewhere in Scripture groaning, praying and bearing witness, and we hesitate to accept that he spoke in this way, because our thoughts are reluctant to descend from our previous contemplation of his divinity to his humiliation. We feel we are almost doing him an injury by acknowledging these words as his, as belonging to the one to whom we were praying when we were praying to God, and we are often tempted to change the meaning of the passage. But Scripture is clear that these passages must be attributed to him and not to another.

So let us be vigilant in our faith, and realize that the one whom we saw previously in the form of God has accepted the form of a servant, made in the image of a human being, and that in this form he humbled himself, becoming obedient unto death. He took as his own the words of the psalmist, as he hung from the cross and said: 'My God, my God, why have you forsaken me?'

Christ prays as a slave, and himself is prayed to as God. He is both creator and creature, himself remaining unchanged, assuming the form of a creature so that creation might be changed, by making us the body and himself the head of one complete human being.

And so we pray to him, through him, in him and with him. We speak in him, and he speaks with and in us the words of this psalm, which is entitled 'A Prayer of David'. This is because our Lord was son of David according to the flesh, but David's Lord with respect to his divine nature, and indeed, David's creator. He existed not only before David, but also before Abraham and Adam from whom all humankind came, and yet further, before the heavens and the earth, in which is contained the whole of creation.

(86)

# *Prudent fear and patience*

The terrors sent by God disturb the faithful in their weakness, for it is prudent to be afraid even if what we fear does not happen in the end. Sometimes these fears are overwhelming like a wave of water, and they torment the mind with a variety of ills. They are to be found at various periods and places in the Church during her pilgrimage through this world, and so the psalmist says 'All day', signifying the passage of time until the end of the world.

We often find that the saints are deserted by their friends and acquaintances whose worldly interests are under threat. About these Paul says: 'All have abandoned me, may they not be blamed for this'. But what is the point of all this if not that the prayer of Christ's holy body the Church, in the morning after her night of infidelity, may in the light of faith bring forward God's work to the present, until our final salvation comes, in hope of which (though not yet in fact) we have been saved, and which we faithfully await in patience?

Then the Lord shall not reject our prayers, since there will be nothing left to ask for, and whatever good thing has been asked for will be given. And God shall not turn away his face from us, for we shall see him as he is. And we shall not be poor, for God himself will be all in all, nor shall we work, for we shall be sufficient. And when we are raised up, we shall not be upset and brought low, for there will be no adversity, and we shall not face God's anger even for a moment, for we shall abide in his loving kindness. And we shall be disturbed by none of his terrors, for we shall be blessed by the promises he has kept, and we shall be surrounded by friends who have no enemy to fear.

*(88)*

# God protects us

'He will cover you between his shoulders, and under his wings you will find hope.' The psalmist says this to stop you trying to find protection by your own resources, from thinking you can be your own protector. It is God who will protect you and deliver you from harsh words and from the hunter's snare.

'He will cover you between his shoulders.' This means protection, before you and behind you, as the shoulders are on each side of the head. He also says: 'and under his wings you will find hope'. This makes it clear that the protection of God's extended wings keeps you between his shoulders, so that enveloping you on both sides they hold you between them. Thus you need not fear lest anyone will hurt you. But do not leave that place of safety which no enemy dare approach. If a hen keeps her young safe under her wings, how much safer you will be under the wings of God, safe against the devil and his angels, those powers of the air who fly around like hawks aiming to seize the weakest chick.

Not without cause is a comparison made between a hen and God's very Wisdom. Christ himself, our Lord and Saviour, tells us he is like a hen: 'Jerusalem, Jerusalem, how often have I wanted to gather your children as a hen gathers her young, and you would not let me'. Jerusalem refused him. Let us accept him. Jerusalem fled from the hen's protecting wings and was seized by the powers of the air. Although she was weak, she presumed on her own strength. Let us acknowledge our weakness and take refuge beneath God's wings. He will be to us like a hen protecting her young.

There is nothing dishonourable in the name of a hen. My brothers and sisters, think of other species of bird. We can see many of them hatching their young and keeping them warm, yet no bird is so vulnerable as the hen when she is with her young. Consider, my beloved. We see swallows, sparrows and storks away from their nests, and we cannot tell whether they have any young. But we recognize the hen by the feebleness of her cry and the loosening of her feathers. She is completely changed by her love for her young. Because they are weak, she shares their weakness. And because we were feeble creatures, God's Wisdom made himself weak for our sakes. Because the Word was made flesh and lived among us, we can find hope under the shadow of his wings.

*(91)*

# Give thanks for God always

It is only the life to come which makes us true Christians. No one should think that worldly happiness or good things in this life will result from being a Christian. They should rather use their present good fortune while it lasts in whatever way and to whatever extent they can. When they have good fortune, they should give thanks for God's compassion. When it is absent, they should give thanks for his righteousness. In all circumstances they should be grateful to their Father when he consoles and comforts them, but also when he corrects and punishes them. For God always loves us whether he consoles or reproves us, and we should repeat what we hear in this psalm: 'It is good to give thanks to the Lord, and sing praises to your name, O Most High'.

*(92)*

# Unite yourself to the eternity of God

'How wonderful are your works, O Lord! Your thoughts are too deep for me to understand.' Now, my brothers and sisters, no ocean is as deep as the mind of God, who inflicts hardship on the good and allows the wicked to flourish. In those deeps are shipwrecked all who lack faith. Do you want to cross these depths? Then do not turn away from the cross of Christ. You shall not sink: hold fast to Christ.

What do I mean by this? To help you hold fast he himself was prepared to suffer hardship on the earth. You have heard in readings from the prophet how he did not turn his shoulders away from the whips, nor his face from men's spittle, nor his cheeks from the blows of their hands. Why should he be willing to undergo all this, unless it was to bring consolation to those who suffer?

He could have waited, and raised his body on the last day, but then you would not have seen him, and would have no grounds for hope. He brought forward his resurrection in time to quell any doubts you might have had. Suffer and endure tribulation in this world, then, and you will reach the same fulfilment as you saw in Christ.

Do not be disturbed by those who do evil and flourish in this world. 'The thoughts of God are too deep for me to understand.' For the present, God has relaxed his control, but later he will tighten the reins. Do not rejoice like the fish which is pleased to taste the bait. The fisherman has not yet drawn tight the hook, but it is already in the fish's mouth. What seems long to you is in truth short, and all things are soon gone. What is the length of a human life compared with God's eternity? Do you want to learn patience? Think of God's everlasting existence.

For as it is you are thinking of your own short lifespan, and you want everything to be fulfilled during your few days on earth. But what is this fulfilment? The glorification of all the good and the damnation of all the wicked. Do you want this to be brought about in your lifetime? God will accomplish it in his own time. So why be weary and impatient? God is eternal, he is long-suffering, and he waits with patience. But you reply, 'I am not long-suffering, for I have to exist in time.' But you have it in your power to unite yourself with the eternity of God, and then you will be a partner in this eternity.

(92)

# Do not be afraid

We read in this psalm: 'Hate evil, you who love the Lord', which is immediately followed by the line: 'The Lord guards the souls of his servants'. This is meant to stop you from being afraid to hate evil in case you are killed for it by the wicked. Listen to Christ, as he guards the souls of his servants and says: 'Do not fear those who can only kill the body but cannot destroy the soul'. They who kill your body have done the most they can, but what is that except what they also did to the Lord your God? Why do you want to possess what Christ possesses if you are afraid to suffer what he suffered? He came to endure your life, bound by time, in weakness, and subject to death.

By all means fear death, if you can avoid having to die. But why not embrace in faith what your nature cannot avoid? Your adversary can threaten to take that life away from you, but God will give you another life as he gave you the first one, which cannot be taken away against his will. But if it is his will that you lose it, he has another life to offer in return. Do not fear to be robbed for his sake.

Are you not prepared to take off patched up clothing? He will give you a garment of glory. What garment am I talking about? 'The corruptible must put on the incorruptible, and the mortal must put on immortality.' Even your body will not perish. The enemy in his raging has power up to the very point of death, but not beyond, and not against the soul, not even against the body. For if he scatters your body he cannot prevent its resurrection.

To people anxious about their souls the Lord says: 'The hairs of your head are all numbered'. How can you be afraid of losing your soul, if you are not even going to lose hair from your head? Everything is numbered by God. He who created everything will restore everything. Humans once did not exist, then they were created. Once they exist, shall they not be restored?

My brothers and sisters, believe this with all your hearts, and 'hate evil, you who love the Lord'. Be strong, not only in loving the Lord, but in hating evil. Let no one frighten you. He who has called you is mightier, for he is all-powerful. He is stronger than every man of strength, and higher than the highest.

God's own Son has died for us. Be sure that you will be given his life to share, you who were given his death as a pledge. For whom did he die? Not for the righteous. Ask Paul: 'And Christ died for sinners'. You were a sinner, and he died for you. Is he going to desert you now that you have been made righteous? He who has justified the unrighteous, shall he now abandon the righteous?

'You who love the Lord, hate evil.' Let no one be afraid. 'The Lord guards the souls of his servants: he will rescue them from the hand of the wicked.'

(97)

# Seeing God the inexpressible

Imitate God in your devotion and think deeply, since God's unseen characteristics may be grasped through the visible things which he has made. Look at what has been created. Wonder at it, and seek its creator. If you are unlike God, you will be cast back, but if you are like him you will rejoice. Being like him, when you begin to approach him and to feel his presence, your love will grow, for God is love.

Then you will begin to sense what you were trying to say and could not put into words. Before you felt the presence of God, you thought you would be able to express his nature, and now, as you begin to feel his presence, you realize that he is inexpressable. But when you have found what you feel cannot be expressed, will you fall silent or will you praise God? Will you fall dumb and fail to give thanks to the One who wants to make himself known to you? You praised God when you were seeking him; so will you be silent now that you have found him? In no way should you show such ingratitude.

Reverence, praise and honour are his. See what you really are: dust and ashes. Consider the One you have been thought worthy to see, and understand that you, a mere human being, have been made capable of seeing God. I am not speaking here of what we deserve, but of what is granted us through the mercy of God.

*(100)*

# Fighting wickedness

'I set no wicked thing before my eyes.' What does this mean? It means that I did not love anything wicked. As you know, a lover is often said to 'keep the beloved before their eyes', and someone who is spurned might complain, 'He does not keep me before his eyes'. What does this mean, to have a person before one's eyes? It means to love them. And what is the absence of love? It is not to have someone in your heart. That is why the psalmist says: 'I set no wicked thing before my eyes', which means, I did not love anything wicked.

He goes on to explain the nature of this wickedness: 'I hated the workers of deception'. Listen, my brothers and sisters, if you walk with Christ in the midst of his house, that is, if you are at peace in your heart or are in the Church itself, making good progress along the path of purity, you should hate not only those liars you find outside its gates, but also any you find within. Who are these liars? They are those who hate the law of God, those who hear it and fail to keep it. These are the ones called liars. So hate the workers of deception. Drive them far way from you. But you ought only to hate them as liars, and not as human beings. A person who is a liar may be designated by two names, 'human' and 'liar'. God created their humanity. They turned themselves into liars.

Show love for that part of them which God has made. Hunt down what is their own creation, and when you have done so, kill the deception, so that what God has created will be set free.

*(101)*

# Praise God even in sleep

God may be said to have ears, just as the heart may be said to have a voice. A person may speak to their inner thoughts and tell them to praise God, saying: 'All my inward parts, bless God's holy name'. These inner parts are your very soul. For the psalmist then says: 'Bless the Lord, my soul, and all that is within me bless his holy name'. Shout these blessings if there is anyone to hear. Keep silent if there is none. But there is always someone who can hear your soul. We began to speak the blessing, and to sing these very words: 'Bless the Lord, my soul, and all that is within me, bless his holy name'. We sang until we had sung enough, and then we fell silent, but should we therefore have ceased from blessing God in the inmost part of our being? Our voices are heard at various times, but the voice of our souls should not cease.

When you gather in Church to sing a hymn, let your voice sing the praises of God. Then, when you have prayed all you can and left Church, let your soul continue to sing the praises of God. You are at work: let your soul praise God. You are eating a meal: hear what St Paul says: 'Whether you are eating or drinking, do everything to the glory of God'. I might even say, praise God in your soul while you are asleep. Do not let yourself be disturbed by any thought of sin, theft, or conspiracy to defraud. Let innocence be your soul's voice even while you sleep. 'Bless the Lord, my soul, and let all that is within me bless his holy name.'

*(103)*

# Spiritual inebriation

'And wine makes glad the human heart.' This does not mean we should now plan to get drunk. But in another sense, we *should* all get drunk. 'How wonderful is your cup of drunkenness.'

So in one sense, we should not forbid drunkenness altogether, indeed, as I say, we *should* get drunk. But we must be aware of where this feeling of drunkenness comes from. I am talking of the feeling that comes from drinking from the wonderful cup of the Lord. The effects of *this* feeling will be seen in your holy love of justice and in the turning of your mind away from earthly things to heaven.

*(104)*

# Trust in God

'The Lord is my strength and praise, and he has become my salvation.' The people who fall down when they are put under pressure are those who wish to be their own strength and praise. The failure of these things causes people to fall in the fight. And so those whose strength and praise is the Lord do not fail, for his strength and praise remain firm. He becomes their salvation, not because of a change in him, but because *they* are changed when they start to believe in him. He does not need to save himself, but he becomes the salvation of those who turn to him, which he was not when they were turned away from him and relied upon themselves.

(118)

# Eternal wealth

The psalmist says: 'Prosperity for those who love you'. He is speaking to Jerusalem herself. Prosperity is for those who love her: freedom from want. Here they are in need, there they shall prosper. Here they are weak, there they are strong. Here they are poor, there they are rich.

But where does their wealth come from? From the fact that they have given away what God gave them on earth, and will then receive for eternity what God shall give them in heaven.

On earth, my brothers and sisters, they are both rich and poor. The rich must acknowledge that they are poor. If they think that they are rich, they are showing pride rather than prosperity. Let them acknowledge that they are empty, so that they can be filled in heaven. What do they have here? Gold. What do they not yet have? Eternal life. Let them think about both what they have and what they do not have. Brothers and sisters, let them give from their abundance, so that they may later receive what they lack. Let them give up what they have in order to buy what they lack. 'Prosperity for those who love you.'

(122)

# Poverty of spirit

True Christians should not be rich, but should recognize that they really are poor. If they have wealth, they should realize that these are not real riches, and should yearn for another kind of wealth. For those who seek the false kind do not seek the true.

Those who seek true wealth do so from a position of poverty, and they are right to say, 'I am poor and in misery'. But someone who is financially poor and also full of wickedness cannot in any sense be said to be rich. Their poverty makes them discontented, and they set against the righteousness of God the self-righteousness which they find in abundance in their own heart.

But how can we be rich in righteousness? However righteous we are, our righteousness is merely spray in comparison to that fountain of righteousness which softens our lives and melts the hardness of our wickedness. All we have to do is desire to be filled from the overflowing fountain of God's righteousness in order to be sated with its richness. The psalm says of that fountain: 'They are drunk from the riches of your house, and you will give them to drink from the torrent of your pleasure'.

But while we are on this earth, we should realize that we are poor and needy; that we lack not only that wealth which is false, but that we are also destitute in respect of our salvation. Even in our physical wholeness let us understand that we are weak. Whatever this body does to overcome its weariness, caused by suffering, thirst and hunger, labouring in wakefulness, standing upright, walking or sitting, it will find yet more weariness. Of itself, the body cannot provide a sufficiency of health. Our bodily satisfactions are not true wealth, but are yet more begging, for the greater they are, the more grows our greed and neediness. There is no bodily health here, but weakness. We are, however, daily refreshed with the medicines that God makes available, simply in that we eat and drink. Brothers and sisters, if you want to know what kind of sickness has us in its grip, consider that someone who goes without food for seven days will starve to death. The disease of hunger is always with us, though we do not notice it because we treat it daily, but its presence is proof that we are not in perfect health . . .

But in the heavenly city there will be true wealth, for there we will really lack nothing. We will not want for anything, and our health will be real. Real health will come when death is swallowed up in victory, and when this corruptible flesh shall put on incorruption, and this mortal body shall put on immortality. Then there will be true health, along with true and perfect righteousness; then we will be incapable of doing, even of contemplating, anything evil. But for the present, in our poverty, need, want and sorrow, we sigh, groan, pray and lift our eyes to God. For we are despised by those who are happy in this world. They have their abundance. And those who are unfortunate in this world despise us as well, for they too have an abundance, but only of false self-righteousness. Filled with this, they cannot achieve the righteousness which is true.

But make sure you want and pray for true righteousness, in order to achieve it, and listen to the Gospel: 'Blessed are those who hunger and thirst after righteousness, for they shall be satisfied'.

*(123)*

112

# *A cry from the depths*

I assume that you are still alert with eyes and heart, and so we may sing with understanding: 'Out of the depths have I cried to you, O Lord; O Lord, hear my voice'. For this is the voice of one who is rising up, and the music is in a gradual measure. Now each one of us needs to see in what depths we lie, from which we cry to God. Jonah cried from the depths, from the belly of the whale. He was not only under the waves, but was also in the beast's stomach. But the whale could not prevent his voice from reaching God, and its belly could not contain his prayer. It broke through everything and reached the ears of God. But we must also understand the depths from which we cry to God.

Our depths are this mortal life. Whoever has realized they are in the depths cries, groans, sighs, until they are lifted out and come to him who sits above all chasms and above the Cherubim, above everything he created, both physical and spiritual. He sits until the soul comes to him, until, as his own image, it is set free by him.

That image belongs to humanity, which is buffeted in these deeps of our mortal life by great waves, and is beaten down into the depths unless it is renewed and restored by God, who marked it with the impression of himself when he created humankind. Human beings were capable of bringing about their own fall, but not their resurrection. So unless the soul is freed by God, it lies for ever in the depths. But when we call from the depths, we rise up, and our cries do not let us stay long down there. Those who do stay in the depths are the ones who do not cry out, as it is written: 'When the sinner reaches the depths of wickedness, he is contemptuous'. You can imagine how deep those depths must be when God is despised.

If a person realized that they are overwhelmed by each day's sin and weighed down by a mass of wrongdoing, they would laugh if you suggested they should pray to God. They would say, 'If my crimes really were displeasing to God, would I still be alive? If God were concerned about human affairs and my terrible misdeeds, could I still not only be alive, but actually prospering?' This kind of thing is said by those who are deep in the mire and doing well in their wickedness. The deeper they go down, the happier they imagine themselves to be. But it is a false happiness, and, in fact, a worse misery than before. Then such people will usually go on to say, 'Since I have committed many crimes, and damnation looms, I shall lose out by not doing whatever is in my power; if from now on I am lost, why should I not do whatever I can?' Indeed, what do the most desperate robbers often say? 'The judge will hang me for one murder as much as for five or ten. Why should I not now commit whatever crime comes into my head?' This is what is meant when it is said: 'When the sinner reaches the depths of wickedness, he is contemptuous'.

But the Lord Jesus Christ, who has not despised our lowliness and who has deigned to enter our lives promising forgiveness of every sin, has roused us even from the depths, so that even under a heap of sins we may cry out, and our voice reach God. And where are we crying from, but from the depths of wickedness?

(130)

# The resurrection

There are those who say: 'Behold the Lord has risen, but can I therefore hope that I will rise?' Yes, indeed. For the Lord rose in a form that he had taken from you. For he would not have risen had he not died, and he would not have died had he not borne our fleshly nature.

What did the Lord take from you? Your fleshly nature. What was he in himself? The Word of God, who was before all things, and through whom all things were made. But the Word took flesh and lived among us, so that he might take something from us, and offer it on our behalf, as does a priest when we want to appease God for our sins.

So in this case, Christ our priest has received from us what he is to offer on our behalf. For he has received from us our fleshly nature, and in that flesh he became a victim, holocaust and sacrifice. In his passion he became a sacrifice, and in his resurrection he restored that which had been killed.

As he gave this your first fruits' sacrifice to God, he said to you: 'Now that everything you are and have has been consecrated to God, since you have offered such first fruits as these to him, you may hope that you too will experience the same resurrection that has already happened for you in those very first fruits.

*(130)*

# God is our bread

What does it mean when it says: 'And her poor will I satisfy with bread'? We must first be poor, and then we shall be satisfied.

But many Christians are proud and place their trust in this world. They may worship Christ, but they are not satisfied with this. For they have already achieved satisfaction elsewhere, and are rich in arrogance. Of such it is said: 'A rebuke to the rich, and contempt for the proud'. They are rich, so they eat, but they are not satisfied. Of them it says in this psalm: 'All the rich of the earth have eaten and worshipped'. They adore, venerate, and beseech Christ, but they are not filled with his wisdom and justice. Why not? Because they are not poor.

The poor, that is those who are humble of heart, eat as they are hungry, and they are hungry because they fail to find nourishment in this world. Someone who has had enough will spew out what you give them because they are full. Give me rather the one who is hungry, of whom it is said: 'Blessed are those who hunger and thirst for justice, for they will be satisfied'. And these are the poor of whom the psalmist says: 'And her poor will I satisfy with bread'. Also, while it says, 'All the rich of the earth have eaten and worshipped', it is elsewhere said of the poor: 'The poor shall eat and be satisfied, and those who seek the Lord shall praise him'.

We are told of the rich eating and worshipping, and also of the poor eating and being satisfied. Why, unlike the rich, are the poor satisfied? What is this satisfaction, and where does it come from? It is from God, for God himself is the bread which is given.

(132)

# Embracing poverty

Be poor, then, be like widows among the members of Christ's body, and do not look for any help except from the one God. Money is nothing, and cannot help you; many, indeed, fall headlong and perish on account of money. And many people have been pursued for their wealth by robbers. They would have been safe had they not possessed what they were being pursued for. And many people have relied on their more powerful friends. Those on whom they relied have fallen and have involved them in their fall.

Look at the examples provided by the human race. You are not being told anything out of the ordinary. The examples do not just come from the Scriptures: you can take them from the world around you. Take care not to rely on money, human friendship, honour, and worldly boasting. Get rid of your reliance. But if you enjoy these benefits, then give thanks to God if you are able to despise them. If, however, you are puffed up, then you need not be anxious about being the prey of other people, for you are already the prey of the devil.

If you do not rely on these benefits, you will be counted among the members of the widowed Church, about which it is said: 'I will cover her widows with blessings', and you will be one of the poor in the saying: 'And her poor will I satisfy with bread'.

·(132)

# The heavenly Jerusalem

Brothers and sisters, continue to play your music even while you work. Sing to each other the songs of Zion. You heard the songs with gladness, so now gladly perform what you have heard. Do not be like the willows of Babylon, fed by her rivers but bearing no fruit. Sigh for the heavenly Jerusalem. For where your hope goes on before, your way of life will follow, and in heaven we shall be with Christ. He is now our head. He now rules us from above. In that city he will gather us to himself, and we shall be equal to the angels of God. By ourselves we would not have dared to imagine this, had not God's Word promised it.

So, my brothers and sisters, fix your desire on this and think about it day and night. Do not presume on whatever favours you may have received from the world. Do not willingly converse with your desires: if your enemy is a great one, kill it against the rock; if it is a small one, dash it against the stones. Let the rock be victorious. Let the rock be your foundation, unless you want to be washed away by flood, wind or rain.

If you want to be armed against the world's temptations, let the desire for the heavenly Jerusalem grow and be strengthened in your hearts. Your captivity will pass and your joy will come. The last enemy will be destroyed, and we shall triumph immortal with our king.

*(137)*

# The beauty of heaven

'That they may make known your might to the children of men, and the glory of the greatness of the beauty of your kingdom.' This is how your saints speak of your kingdom. Your kingdom has beauty in great abundance. Whatever has beauty on earth takes it from you. What kind of beauty, then, can be found in heaven?

We should not let this frighten us, for it will be a beauty in which we can take delight. What is this beauty, which the saints will enjoy when it is said to them: 'Come, you blessed ones of my Father, hold fast to the kingdom'? Where will they go, and where have they come from? My brothers and sisters, think about this beauty as hard as you can, the beauty of that kingdom which is to come, of which the prayer says: 'Thy kingdom come'. We want the kingdom to come. The saints preach that it will come.

Consider this world of ours. It has a certain beauty. Is there not beauty in the earth, the sea, the air, the sky and the stars, and are we not moved by awe when we consider them? Does this beauty not make it seem as if nothing more beautiful could be found? But here amidst this almost unutterable beauty and loveliness there live among you worms and mice and all the earth's creeping vermin. So what degree of beauty will we find in heaven, where only the angels will be living among us?

It would not have been enough when speaking of heaven to mention the 'glory of its beauty', for one could have used these words of any earthly beauty, of the greenness of the earth or the gleaming glory of the sky. Instead, it says: 'Of the greatness of the glory of your kingdom', which indicates something we believe in as not yet seen, but in our belief we desire to see it, and in our desire to possess it, we endure all hardships.

The beauty of heaven is a great beauty, and so let us love it before we see it, so that once we have seen it we may hold fast to it.

*(145)*

# *Praising God with the whole of your life*

So now, brothers and sisters, I call on you to praise God, which is what we tell each other to do when we say 'Alleluia'. You say 'praise God' to another, and they say the same to you. When all encourage each other, then all are doing what they encourage others to do.

But you must praise God with your whole being, not just with your tongue and the sound of your voice: praise him with your conscience, your actions, your way of life. If we praise God only when we are gathered in church, we will stop praising God every time we go home. Live a good life, and persevere in it, and you will always be praising God; you cease to praise God when you stop acting justly and doing what pleases him.

For if you keep to a good way of life, your tongue may stay silent, but your whole life will cry out with praises, and the ears of God will listen to your heart. Our ears are receptive to voices, just as the ears of God are receptive to our hearts.

Good thoughts cannot bring about evil actions. For actions proceed from the thought. No one can do anything, or make their limbs perform any action unless a mental command has come first. In the same way the emperor's command goes out from the palace and over the whole Roman empire, and you can see it taking effect in the provinces. An enormous effect follows one simple order that comes from the emperor sitting inside his palace. When he speaks he is only moving his lips, but the whole province is affected when his orders are carried out. So in each person there sits an interior principle of command in the heart. If it commands good things, they are done. If it commands evil things, they too are done.

When Christ sits in that place of command, what else can he order but what is good? When the devil sits there in possession, what can he order but evil? It is God's will that you should have the choice of preparing a place for God or for the devil. When you have prepared it, the one who occupies it will be the one who issues the commands.

So, brothers and sisters, do not think only about the sounds you are making. When you praise God, praise him with your whole being. Let your voice, your actions and your life itself sing out in praise.

*(149)*

# The sacrifice of God

'Let the children of Zion exult in their king.' The children of the Church are Israel. Zion was a kingdom that fell, and in its ruins there lived a holy people for a time, but the true Zion and the true Jerusalem (for Zion is Jerusalem) is in heaven, and is our mother. She herself gave us birth, she herself is the Church of the holy ones, she herself has fed us.

In part she is a pilgrim church, but mostly she is to be found in heaven. From the heavenly part come the blessed angels, and from the pilgrim part still on this earth comes the hope of the righteous. From the first part comes the cry, 'Glory to God in the highest', and from the second, 'And on earth peace to people of good will'.

So those who are groaning in this life and yearning for the land of heaven should run towards it – with love, that is, not with their feet. And let them take not a ship but wings, the two wings of love, the two wings that are love of God and love of our neighbour. For we are pilgrims, we sigh and we groan . . .

'Let Israel rejoice in the one who made him, and let the children of Zion exult in their king.' The 'children of Zion' are the same as Israel, and the king is the same as 'the one who made him'. The one who made us was the Son of God, and he was also made one of us. He ruled over us as our king because as our creator he made us. He is the one through whom we were made, the one through whom we are ruled. And so we are called Christians because he is the Christ. He is called Christ from his chrism or anointing. Kings and priests were the ones who were anointed, and Christ was rightly anointed as king and priest. As king he has fought for us and as priest he has offered himself on our behalf. When he fought for us it seemed that he had been defeated, but in truth the victory was his. For he was crucified, and from the cross on which he had been fastened, he slew the devil: hence he is our king. Whence comes his priesthood? From the fact that he offered himself for us.

'Give this priest what he offers.' But what pure victim could a human being find to give? What pure gift could a sinner bring? In your immorality and wickedness whatever you bring is unclean, and something pure must be offered on your behalf.

See what you have to offer: you will not find anything. God takes no delight in rams, goats or bulls. They all belong to him even if you do not offer them. So offer him a pure sacrifice. But you are a sinner, you are irreligious, you have an unclean conscience. Perhaps you could be purified, and then you could offer something pure, but for you to be purified, something pure first has to be offered on your behalf. What can you offer? If you have been purified you can offer something pure. So the priest who is pure offers himself and will purify you. This is what Christ has done. He finds in humanity nothing pure that he can offer on our behalf, so he has offered himself as a pure victim. O blessed and true victim, unstained gift!

Now he did not offer what we had given him without first making it pure. For he received his fleshly human nature from us, and offered it. He received it from the womb of the Virgin Mary, so that he might offer pure flesh on behalf of the impure. He himself is our priest and king, and in him we should rejoice.

(149)